Pet Me Safely

I love to be petted, hugged and loved.
But some dogs do not like strangers.

Dogs do not think about you the
same way people do. This book can
help you learn how to pet dogs safely.

1

Published and distributed by
Legacy Publishers LLC
1866 Oak Harbor Drive SW
Ocean Isle Beach NC 28469
Toll-free Phone: 1.800.290.8055

E-mail: mrcofer@amadeusbooks.com
website: www.amadeusbooks.com

Printed in China
ISBN 978-1-932957-08-1

First Printing

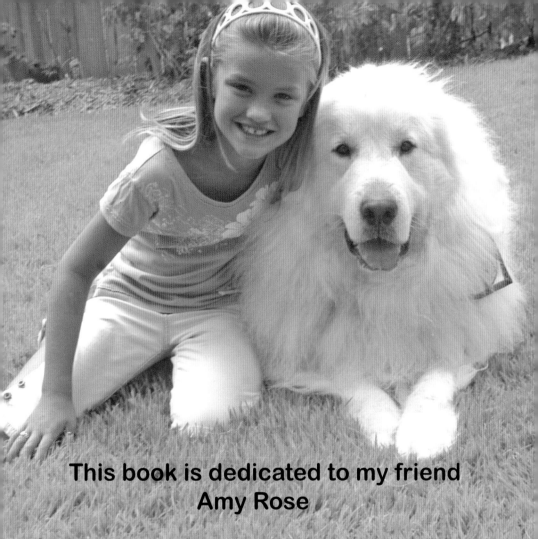

This book is dedicated to my friend
Amy Rose

My name is Amadeus. Say it like this: "Ah-muh-day-us."
I am a Great Pyrenees Mountain Dog.
I am a Therapy Dog, certified by
the American Kennel Club
as a Canine Good Citizen.

Find games and puzzles and more on my website
www.amadeusbooks.com

This book belongs to:

_____

Amadeus the Traveling Dog

The first safety rule in petting a dog is to always ask permission from the owner before petting any dog. Some dogs are not friendly.

6

Even grandparents should ask if the dog is friendly before petting him.

Walk quietly up to my side first,
not in front of me. Some dogs think
you are a bully if you come to their
face first and look them in the eyes.

Some people need help coming up to my side. I try to stand very still so I won't get in their way.

Let me smell your hand.
That is how I get to know you.
Make a fist or keep your hand
open and your fingers close
together. Hold your hand
under my nose.

10

If you want to pat me on the head, do it from my side. Do not reach your hand across my face. In the dog world, reaching your hand across a dog's face is rude. It is OK if I turn my head to say "Hello."

Pet me under the chin. Scratch me gently behind the ears.
Be kind. Never pull my hair, ears or tail. Be careful not to
jump on my back or step on my feet. Sudden actions can
make a dog nervous.

Pet me along the back or sides between my ears and tail. Stroke from the head toward the tail. This is the direction in which my hair grows. Be careful not to stroke against the hair because that can make some dogs think you are a bully.

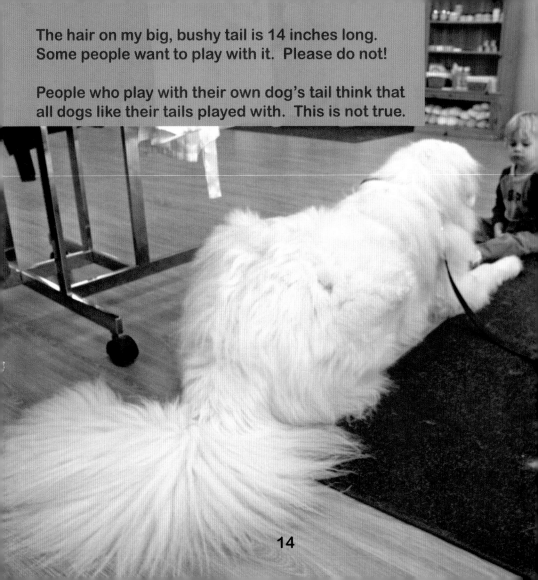

The hair on my big, bushy tail is 14 inches long. Some people want to play with it. Please do not!

People who play with their own dog's tail think that all dogs like their tails played with. This is not true.

14

Many dogs think you are trying to be a bully when you play with their tails. They may move away, growl, or even snap at you. Penny, my pet cat, knows that. She waited until I was fast asleep.

I like to be hugged.
Hug me gently.

16

Be careful not to squeeze too tightly. You could hurt me.

If a dog thinks you are trying to hurt him, he may growl at you.

17

Some people like to kiss me. I may kiss them back.

Be careful when kissing dogs. Some dogs may not like your face so close to theirs. Ask the owner if the dog likes to be kissed.

18

People often call me a teddy bear dog because I am so soft and cuddly.

19

I like to play games with my friends. I love soccer and wheelchair basketball. I chase the ball and bring it back to my friends.

But there are some games you should never play with a dog, like tug-of-war. The dog can easily get too excited. He can start to think of you as another dog and play too rough.

Some people like to "play puppy" with their dogs. This can be a dangerous game, especially if you are face-to-face with the dog. Dogs often nip and snap at each other while playing together.

21

When getting a good ear scratch,
I like to lean in for more.

I give my books to sick children when I
visit them at a hospital. They read to me
and tell me their stories while petting me.

Dogs are great listeners.

23

I can shake your hand when I meet you.
Just put out your hand and say,
"Amadeus, shake" or "Give me paw."

Teach your dog to shake hands.

24

I may roll over on my back and ask for a tummy rub. Gently rub
my chest and neck area.   Do not rub the lower part of my tummy
because you could hurt me.

Some kids treat me like a big, white fluffy pillow. If I get tired of this, I will get up and walk away. Some dogs do not like to be used as a pillow. Choose your pet pillows carefully.

26

Even a nice dog can get tired. Dogs may let you know when they want to be left alone by walking away. If you ever hear a dog go "Grrrr" with a low growl in its throat, back away. It is a warning before the dog bites.

Miss Mary, my trainer, taught me to never accept food or water from strangers. Always ask the owner before offering food to a dog. Many dogs would growl at you for putting your hand in their food bowl.

28

Never try to pet a dog when he is eating or drinking. He may think you are trying to get his food or water.

Never pet a dog while he is chewing on a bone or toy. He may think you are trying to take it away.

Never try to pet me when I am asleep. I may be having a bad dream and think you are part of the dream.

Just take a picture of me instead. When I wake up, I will be in a better mood to play with you.

31

I love to be around lots of children. I visit libraries, classrooms and auditoriums. Some dogs get nervous when there is a lot of noise, but not me.

32

Some dogs get nervous when surrounded by a lot of people, especially if they are all trying to pet him at once. Give the dog extra room to breathe so he does not feel closed in.

The best way to keep a dog from chasing you is to stand still. If you run, he may chase you. Pretend you are a tree. Fold your arms over your chest and stand still.

Do not look directly at the dog. Watch him out of the corner of your eye. the dog will think that you are not a threat and go away.

If a dog starts to bother you, protect your face. Pretend to be a rock. Squat down on the ground and put your face down by your knees. Cover your head with your hands. Be very still. The dog will usually get bored and leave you alone.

Now that you know how to pet dogs safely, practice what you learned. Teach your friends how to behave safely around dogs. Dogs can be your best friends!